FRANCIS FRITH'S

CARDIFF
OLD AND NEW

PHOTOGRAPHIC MEMORIES

MARK ISAACS was born, raised and educated in Cardiff. He lives in the Roath area of the city with his wife and young son. He has an honours degree in Art Education, and has worked for the libraries in Cardiff for 16 years. As well as local history, his interests (in no particular order) include: Cardiff City Football Club, 70's Punk music, rockabilly, history of fashion, modern design and architecture and vintage wristwatches. He is a self-confessed hoarder of books, magazines and memorabilia. He dedicates this book to Daniel Wynn Isaacs – a young Cardiffian.

FRANCIS FRITH'S
PHOTOGRAPHIC MEMORIES

CARDIFF
OLD AND NEW

PHOTOGRAPHIC MEMORIES

MARK ISAACS

First published in the United Kingdom in 2004 by
Frith Book Company Ltd

Limited Hardback Subscribers Edition Published in 2004
ISBN 1-85937-928-1

Paperback Edition 2004
ISBN 1-85937-791-2

British Library Cataloguing in Publication Data

Francis Frith's Cardiff Old and New - Photographic Memories
Mark Isaacs

Frith Book Company Ltd
Frith's Barn, Teffont,
Salisbury, Wiltshire SP3 5QP
Tel: +44 (0) 1722 716 376
Email: info@francisfrith.co.uk
www.francisfrith.co.uk

Printed and bound in Great Britain

Front Cover: **CARDIFF**, *Queen Street 1902* 48997
Frontispiece: **CARDIFF**, *St Mary Street 1893* 32677

2004 images by Michael Cutter

*The colour-tinting is for illustrative purposes only, and is not intended to
be historically accurate*

AS WITH ANY HISTORICAL DATABASE THE FRITH ARCHIVE IS
CONSTANTLY BEING CORRECTED AND IMPROVED AND THE
PUBLISHERS WOULD WELCOME INFORMATION ON OMISSIONS OR INACCU-
RACIES

CONTENTS

FRANCIS FRITH
VICTORIAN PIONEER

FRANCIS FRITH, founder of the world-famous photographic archive, was a complex and multi-talented man. A devout Quaker and a highly successful Victorian businessman, he was philosophical by nature and pioneering in outlook.

By 1855 he had already established a wholesale grocery business in Liverpool, and sold it for the astonishing sum of £200,000, which is the equivalent today of over £15,000,000. Now a very rich man, he was able to indulge his passion for travel. As a child he had pored over travel books written by early explorers, and his fancy and imagination had been stirred by family holidays to the sublime mountain regions of Wales and Scotland. 'What lands of spirit-stirring and enriching scenes and places!' he had written. He was to return to these scenes of grandeur in later years to 'recapture the thousands of vivid and tender memories', but with a different purpose. Now in his thirties, and captivated by the new science of photography, Frith set out on a series of pioneering journeys up the Nile and to the Near East that occupied him from 1856 until 1860.

INTRIGUE AND EXPLORATION

These far-flung journeys were packed with intrigue and adventure. In his life story, written when he was sixty-three, Frith tells of being held captive by bandits, and of fighting 'an awful midnight battle to the very point of surrender with a deadly pack of hungry, wild dogs'. Wearing flowing Arab costume, Frith arrived at Akaba by camel sixty years before Lawrence of Arabia, where he encountered 'desert princes and rival sheikhs, blazing with jewel-hilted swords'.

He was the first photographer to venture beyond the sixth cataract of the Nile. Africa was still the mysterious 'Dark Continent', and Stanley and Livingstone's historic meeting was a decade into the future. The conditions for picture taking confound belief. He laboured for hours in his wicker dark-room in the sweltering heat of the desert, while the volatile chemicals fizzed dangerously in their trays. Back in London he exhibited his photographs and was 'rapturously cheered' by members of the Royal Society. His reputation as a photographer was made overnight.

VENTURE OF A LIFE-TIME

Characteristically, Frith quickly spotted the opportunity to create a new business as a specialist publisher of photographs. He lived in an era of immense and sometimes violent change.

For the poor in the early part of Victoria's reign work was exhausting and the hours long, and people had precious little free time to enjoy themselves. Most had no transport other than a cart or gig at their disposal, and rarely travelled far beyond the boundaries of their own town or village. However, by the 1870s the railways had threaded their way across the country, and Bank Holidays and half-day Saturdays had been made obligatory by Act of Parliament. All of a sudden the working man and his family were able to enjoy days out and see a little more of the world.

With typical business acumen, Francis Frith foresaw that these new tourists would enjoy having souvenirs to commemorate their days out. In 1860 he married Mary Ann Rosling and set out on a new career: his aim was to photograph every city, town and village in Britain. For the next thirty years he travelled the country by train and by pony and trap, producing fine photographs of seaside resorts and beauty spots that were keenly bought by millions of Victorians. These prints were painstakingly pasted into family albums and pored over during the dark nights of winter, rekindling precious memories of summer excursions.

THE RISE OF FRITH & CO

Frith's studio was soon supplying retail shops all over the country. To meet the demand he gathered about him a small team of photographers, and published the work of independent artist-photographers of the calibre of Roger Fenton and Francis Bedford. In order to gain some understanding of the scale of Frith's business one only has to look at the catalogue issued by Frith & Co in 1886: it runs to some 670 pages, listing not only many thousands of views of the British Isles but also many photographs of most European countries, and China, Japan, the USA and Canada - note the sample page shown on page 9 from the hand-written Frith & Co ledgers recording the pictures. By 1890 Frith had created the greatest specialist photographic publishing company in the world, with over 2,000 sales outlets - more than the combined number that Boots and WH Smith have today! The picture on the next page shows the Frith & Co display board at Ingleton in the Yorkshire Dales (left of window). Beautifully constructed with a mahogany frame and gilt inserts, it could display up to a dozen local scenes.

POSTCARD BONANZA

The ever-popular holiday postcard we know today took many years to develop. In 1870 the Post Office issued the first plain cards, with a pre-printed stamp on one face. In 1894 they allowed other publishers' cards to be sent through the mail with an attached adhesive halfpenny stamp. Demand grew rapidly, and in 1895 a new size of postcard was permitted called the court card, but there was little room for illustration. In 1899, a year after Frith's death, a new card measuring 5.5 x 3.5 inches became the standard format, but it was not until 1902 that the divided back came into being, so that the address and message could be on one face and a full-size illustration on the other. Frith & Co were in the vanguard of postcard development: Frith's sons Eustace and Cyril continued their father's monumental task, expanding the number of views offered to the public and recording more and more places in Britain, as the

5			
6	St Catherine's College	+	
7	Senate House & Library	+	
8		+	
9	Gerrard Hostel Bridge	+ + + +
3 0	Geological Museum	
1	Addenbrooke's Hospital	+
2	St Mary's Church	+
3	Fitzwilliam Museum, Pitt Press &c	+
4		+
5	Buxton, The Crescent	+
6	The Colonnade	+
7	Public Gardens	+
8		+
9	Haddon Hall, View from the Terrace	+
4 0	Miller's Dale	+

coasts and countryside were opened up to mass travel.

Francis Frith had died in 1898 at his villa in Cannes, his great project still growing. The archive he created continued in business for another seventy years. By 1970 it contained over a third of a million pictures showing 7,000 British towns and villages.

FRANCIS FRITH'S LEGACY

Frith's legacy to us today is of immense significance and value, for the magnificent archive of evocative photographs he created provides a unique record of change in the cities, towns and villages throughout Britain over a century and more. Frith and his fellow studio photographers revisited locations many times down the years to update their views, compiling for us an enthralling and colourful pageant of British life and character.

We are fortunate that Frith was dedicated to recording the minutiae of everyday life. For it is this sheer wealth of visual data, the painstaking chronicle of changes in dress, transport, street layouts, buildings, housing, engineering and landscape that captivates us so much today. His remarkable images offer us a powerful link with the past and with the lives of our ancestors.

THE VALUE OF THE ARCHIVE TODAY

Computers have now made it possible for Frith's many thousands of images to be accessed almost instantly. Frith's images are increasingly used as visual resources, by social historians, by researchers into genealogy and ancestry, by architects and town planners, and by teachers involved in local history projects.

In addition, the archive offers every one of us an opportunity to examine the places where we and our families have lived and worked down the years. Highly successful in Frith's own era, the archive is now, a century and more on, entering a new phase of popularity. Historians consider the Francis Frith Collection to be of prime national importance. It is the only archive of its kind remaining in private ownership. Francis Frith's archive is now housed in an historic timber barn in the beautiful village of Teffont in Wiltshire. Its founder would not recognize the archive office as it is today. In place of the many thousands of dusty boxes containing glass plate negatives and an all-pervading odour of photographic chemicals, there are now ranks of computer screens. He would be amazed to watch his images travelling round the world at unimaginable speeds through internet lines.

The archive's future is both bright and exciting. Francis Frith, with his unshakeable belief in making photographs available to the greatest number of people, would undoubtedly approve of what is being done today with his lifetime's work. His photographs depicting our shared past are now bringing pleasure and enlightenment to millions around the world a century and more after his death.

CARDIFF
OLD AND NEW

AN INTRODUCTION

THE YEAR 2004 marks the verge of two extremely significant anniversaries for the City of Cardiff. Here, perhaps, the use of the old cliché 'a once in a lifetime experience' is legitimate. In 2005 it will be 100 years since the granting of city status and 50 since that city was officially recognised as the 'capital of Wales' - the cultural and administrative centre of the nation. At the time of writing this book, the anticipation of the celebrations is palpable and the organisational momentum gathers apace. The build up in the local press has begun, initial arrangements made for civic ceremonies and, like Chinese whispers, rumours abound amongst the city's workers and schoolchildren of a day of public holiday to mark the occasion.

With this in mind it seems quite apt to be travelling back through time to view the city's past via this collection of photographic memories. By way of contrast our inclusion of photographs of today's Cardiff will not only illustrate the profound changes that have taken place since the end of the 19th century, but in many instances will show how very little has altered at all.

'The History of Cardiff' - now that's quite a tricky subject. Some academics claim that there is no definitive history of anything but rather a tapestry of interconnecting viewpoints. For some, history is the life of the common man buffeted and shaped by market forces; for others, men of destiny guided by fate. But what of Cardiff? For a city so relatively small and compact, its story is broad and complex enough to encompass the ancient, the not so ancient and the thoroughly modern. The tale of its development has been pushed and cemented together like the outer walls of Cardiff Castle; each century builds its own layer upon the last. When we examine that façade with its varying stones we witness the striations of history. The city with which we are familiar is so inextricably linked with the Marquesses of Bute and their wealth that an historical time chart of the city could be rightly divided into 'BB' and 'AB' sections - 'Before Bute' and 'After Bute ' respectively. If it is true that history is written by the victorious then it is certain that the Bute family name still courses through the city streets.

The story of transition from Roman encampment to 21st-century city is a long and fascinating one and I believe its full exposition is not best served in an introduction such as this.

Many authors have covered this ground admirably and in justifiably great detail. William Rees' book of 1962 is a personal favourite but a host of others have subsequently tackled the subject with great aplomb. Neither do I intend to elaborate at length here on the Butes and their legacy. Their contribution to the city is immeasurable and still tangible today.

The earliest photographs in our collection date from the closing decades of the 19th century. They depict the town in its Victorian pomp; the third Marquess at the height of his influence. I hope that the images and their captions convey something of the grandeur and dynamism of those pivotal years - the modern city in embryo. They must also beg the question of how the industrial-age town came into being - what of Cardiff 'Before Bute'? The incredible progress of the town during the Victorian era can often overshadow its early history. To set the scene for our photographic journey it would be amiss if we were not to recall the ancient foundations of the 19th and 20th century 'Coalopolis'.

In the most basic terms the history of Cardiff can be understood as a repetitive cycle of growth, stability, decline and eventual renewal. The earliest period of growth dates back to the Roman invasion of Britain. What we now know as Cardiff was then a fishing village and had been so since ancient times. The Roman settlers were to erect a fort on the site of today's castle sometime between AD50 and 75. It is quite possible, though not conclusively proven, that 'Cardiff' is derived from 'Caer Didi' - 'Fort of (Roman General) Didius'. Along with the empire the fortunes of the stronghold waxed and waned until the fort was eventually abandoned at the end of the 4th century heralding a period of stagnation for the 'town'. The Norman Conquest led Robert Fitzhamon, a kinsman of William the Conqueror, into South Wales. In around 1090 he established a wooden castle inside the walls of the old Roman fort from which to exert his power. A more substantial stone construction soon replaced the wooden and by the 13th century a protective stone wall had been built around the

CARDIFF, *City Hall and Law Courts 1906* 54938

perimeter of the emerging town which was by now under the control of the De Clare family. During the Middle Ages a population of nearly 2,000 clustered around the castle enjoying the relative peace and prosperity. Local crafts thrived and the town hosted popular markets and fairs. Most significantly, cargo ships made increasing use of the town quay. In 1404 (the same year as the sitting of his first Welsh Parliament), Owain Glyndwr attacked the 'English' town burning much of it to the ground. A subsequent period of renewal saw to its reconstruction.

During the next two centuries Cardiff was to remain a small, relatively insignificant provincial town. The English influence in the region, already dominant, was to be reinforced by the Act of Union in 1536 but concurrent relaxation of punitive restrictions enabled the Welsh themselves to migrate to the town to live and ply their trades. The Second Act of Union allowed the creation of the Shire of Glamorgan with Cardiff as its county town. Cardiff's favourable geographical position allowed the port to handle increasing amounts of import and export trade including small quantities of iron and coal. A certain notoriety began to attach itself too, with the port gaining a reputation for criminal activity with piracy at its core. The Herbert family began to gain prominence in the town and their sponsorship of building work included major restoration of the castle. The tumultuous years of the English Civil War saw the majority of the town backing the Royalist cause but as the tide turned in favour of the Parliamentary forces local support for the King was to waiver. In 1645 Charles I himself visited Cardiff in a vain attempt to raise finance but the town was soon to fall into Parliamentary hands. The last major battle in

Wales took place at St Fagans in 1648 with Parliament's men triumphant.

The days of conflict passed, the town was once more to slide into a period of deep stagnation. Its infrastructure decaying through neglect, Cardiff appeared to be in a state of regression. In 1801 the population was a mere 1,870 - actually less than that of the medieval town. To quantify this inertia one only has to see Swansea with a population of 6,000 at this time with Merthyr boasting an impressive 7,700. As a port Cardiff ranked only alongside Aberthaw and Chepstow. The town was arguably at its lowest ebb but it had one great asset not yet fully exploited - its prime channel coast location. The dark before the dawn? Quite possibly. The closing decades of the 18th century were to usher in such dramatic innovation and development that the fortunes of this backwater town would revive and flourish in such tremendous fashion that for a period it would become one of the most talked about and significant industrial towns in the world. The sea change affected by the nascent Industrial Revolution and the arrival in South Wales of John, Lord Mountstuart in 1776 pushes our chronology into the 'After Bute' era. Here our story of the town's historical stepping stones draws to a close as our photographs of the 'modern metropolis' take over. Suffice it to say that by 1794 the vital canal link between Merthyr and Cardiff was complete facilitating the swift transportation of the precious coal cargo to the coast for export. With the first of the town's iconic docks opened in 1838 it is quite staggering to realise that by 1901 Cardiff's population had risen almost a hundredfold in just 100 years.

Once again we pose the question 'What of Cardiff?' but now, nearing conclusion, we consider, albeit briefly, the ambience and identity of the city today. These are indeed heady times. During the latter years of the last century and the early years of this, the city has enjoyed a sustained period of prosperity and renewal not experienced for 100 years. There are certainly parallels between the epoch-making Victorian Cardiff in all its brash glory and now. Once more the city is a mecca for migration and settlement. Today though it welcomes incomers in pursuit of its first class leisure, recreational and accommodation facilities in both the 'old town' and in the remarkable vision of the reclaimed waterfront with which it is so rightly reunited. Cardiff is now considered one of THE places to live in the United Kingdom with its quality of life/work ratio so consistently high. It's worth remembering that only 25 years ago this proposition would have been sadly implausible.

It is often remarked that Cardiff is a city of contradictions. This judgement may appear to be negative but this benign schizophrenia has facilitated the cultural diversity that we now enjoy. Like most major British ports the city has attracted, absorbed and nurtured incomers of all nationalities in an urban amalgamation of cultures, attitudes and religious beliefs. With historically little tension and conflict the reasons for our enduringly harmonious interrelationship would take social historians a lifetime to analyse.

Are we an English-leaning city in Wales built with Scottish money with a famously international population? Detractors argue that Cardiff is the most anglicised conurbation in Wales, finding it ironic, or worse still incomprehensible, that the city is the capital. This hostility isn't new. In the 19th century certain English Liberals dismissed Cardiff as (the politically right-leaning) Bute's 'Scottish Colony'. In 1955 the tremors of anger and resentment emanating from Swansea could almost be felt inside the walls of City Hall as their anticipated failure to become the Welsh

CARDIFF, *City Hall and Law Courts 2004* C23743k

capital was finally made official. Again Cardiff's 'Welshness' was called into question. The city was mocked as the 'CAPITAL of Wales' - big business and greed overtly influencing its selection.

Cardiff as 'unrepresentative' of Wales? One wonders how representative London is of the rest of England. National identity is certainly an issue. The concept of 'Welshness' rests uneasily on the shoulders of some Cardiffians. On occasion overheard conversations may cause the unwary to think that the rest of South Wales is regarded as a foreign country! This is a deep-rooted civic pride, not ignorance. Language is no doubt an issue with an uneasiness felt by some solely English speakers in regard to their inability to converse in their 'native tongue'. Make no mistake though, the true Cardiffians, regardless of background, are also fiercely patriotic Welshmen or women. A passion for their city can sometimes appear to push 'nationality' into second place. Their 'Welshness' (the definition of which I gladly leave to the individual) may be felt and expressed in seemingly different ways to that of their fellow countrymen but it is none the less real. Witness any international sporting event in the city for proof.

So there it is. My aim has been to briefly give the reader a flavour of the city and to share some impressions of its past and its people. If I have been able to communicate the slightest nuance of feeling that Cardiffians have for their home - a city they regard as unique - then I have been successful. With your appetite hopefully whetted please now waste no time before diving into the fabulous photographs!

CARDIFF, *National Assembly 2004* C23711k

CENTRAL STREETS AND LANDMARKS

CARDIFF, *General View 1893* 32663

In the year of the birth of one of the city's most famous sons, Ivor Novello, we look south down St Mary Street towards Butetown and the docks on the horizon. This is the Cardiff soon 'proud to be a Victorian city'. In the middle distance, road gives way to canal surmounted by a railway bridge - a fitting metaphor for the transport infrastructure so vital to the increasing prosperity of this 'Coalopolis'. Only 20 years have elapsed since census returns show for the first time that the town is the most populous in Wales. Of note are the twin domes of the Western Mail building (centre). Later this year the building would be severely damaged by fire.

▼ **CARDIFF**, *General View 1893* 32665

From the same vantage point as 32663 we now look northwards. With blissful symmetry the horizon here is occupied by Cardiff Castle - the iconic home of the Bute family, facilitators of the modern city and much of its wealth. From here and through 32663 one can trace an imaginary route of influence flowing from the castle, across the town then via the docks and on to the sea. Landmarks ancient and modern, still familiar to us today, cluster on the right of the picture. These include St John's Church, Howell's store and the Cottage public house. At left is Westgate Street where only 40 years earlier ran the course of the Taff. The Cardiff and County Club, later to find a home here, is a new venture founded only three years previously.

► **CARDIFF**
St Mary Street 1893 32677

The photographer has certainly attracted a sizeable group of curious onlookers in this scene dominated by James Howell's store (right). The draper's original Cardiff premises opened in the Hayes in 1865 employing a mere five assistants. Relocating to St Mary Street in 1867 and the shrewd acquisition of adjoining premises allowed the frontage that we see here, constructed in 1879. Only a year prior to our photograph the store expanded 'inwardly' to Trinity Street. The farmer's son from Pembrokeshire was on course to create Wales' premier department store.

◄ **CARDIFF**
St Mary Street 1893 32674

The prosperity of the town is evident in its grand commercial frontage. The theatres Royal and Philharmonic (left) flank the Victoria Tea Company, here perhaps taking delivery from the horse-drawn cart outside. A rival tea merchant, Broomhall and Company, trade just three doors down. An ecclesiastical echo of Cardiff's past is also situated on this busy block - St Mary's Vestry Hall, some 50 years after the church's 'relocation'.

► **CARDIFF**
St Mary Street 1893
32675

The view shows an abundance of public houses and hotels. At far right three stand side by side - the Theatre Royal, then Clarence and (out of picture) the Cambrian. They in turn are overshadowed by the much larger Royal Hotel across the street. The original building (with canopied entrance) opened in 1866, with its façade in the Italian Renaissance style. Lack of capacity precipitated the huge Wood Street corner extension of 1890.

CARDIFF
St Mary Street 2004
C23730k

No longer offering accommodation, the old Royal Hotel premises now operates as a large public house. The most significant recent development in the street however is the Brewery Quarter. The Albert has given way to the Yard and clearance of the old Brains Brewery site has facilitated construction of both restaurant and luxury residential space. A new pedestrian walkway through to Caroline Street bisects the area.

CARDIFF, *St Mary Street 1896* 38709

The landmark Great Western Hotel of 1876, its curved façade created by Blessey in a fantastic French medieval style with Gothic window decoration, draws one's gaze into the commercial hubbub of the street. The same year also saw the opening of the Philharmonic Hall also visible. In the foreground, obscuring a tram, is the Second Marquess' statue which was moved to this location from High Street in 1879.

CARDIFF
St Mary Street 2004
C23731k

Sharp-eyed observers will notice that the conical rooftop spires of the old Great Western building have been removed. Much more obvious is the disappearance of the Marquess' statue - Bute Square is now its third location. Accommodation is again available in this section of the street; a Travelodge nestles next to the Bush Pig public house. Much of the street's visible upper level frontage remains pleasingly unaltered.

CARDIFF, *St Mary Street c1955* C23160

The street familiar today is clearly much in place by the mid 1950s. Westminster House (left) is the only post war addition on view. Power cables for trolley buses and gaps in the pedestrian island evoke this era of road transport. The long defunct Martins Bank echoes this period. In the centre stands Howell's 1930s extension - a stylish addition much lauded by architecture and design historians.

► **CARDIFF**
St Mary Street
2004 C23729k

The road uncannily devoid of traffic, the urban landscape has changed little from that seen in C23160 (page19). The bus shelters (left) are perhaps the most conspicuous addition. Cardiff institutions such as the Indoor Market and the Louis Restaurant occupy their familiar sites. The upper façade visible remains virtually unaltered over the intervening years. The 1970s concrete-fronted Golate House opposite the Sandringham Hotel perhaps the only exception.

◄ **CARDIFF**
High Street 1925
77427

A safe haven for cyclists on a sunny day - some manage to ride two abreast toward the photographer. The shop on the extreme right complete with elegant spherical lighting is Dale, Forty & Co Ltd. As retailers of pianos, organs and gramophones they faced stiff competition from their rivals Thompson & Shackell whose two Cardiff branches underpinned their dominance of the South Wales market.

▲ **CARDIFF,** *High Street 2004* C23726k

Newcomers to the city often blur the distinction between St Mary Street and High Street pictured here. 'Modern' building developments oppose each other on the corners of Church Street and Quay Street but little else has changed architecturally. Note the beautifully ornate entrance to High Street Arcade (left). The sign, just visible extreme right, fittingly proclaims 'Cardiff: City of Arcades'.

◄ **CARDIFF**
High Street c1955
C23163

At this time Cardiff was a city slowly emerging from the austerity of the immediate post war era. At left, in line with the Lyons van, is the entrance to the Castle Arcade - a true gem amongst Cardiff's rich assortment of arcades. Opened in 1887, and entered below Albert Chambers, its remarkable galleried top floor is linked via a network of footbridges to create a labyrinth of small shops.

CARDIFF
High Street 2004
C23727k

Still a busy intersection, the traffic crawls and tourists throng on departing the castle. The public house (left) first opened as the Blue Bell in 1813. Its recent change of name to the rather less gentle sounding Goat Major is in tribute to strong Welsh regimental links to the city. Despite re-branding it remains a 'traditional' pub - increasingly scarce in the city centre.

CARDIFF
Queen Street 1893
32678

The open aspect of the
street pictured here and
familiar to us today
originates from the
demolition of older
buildings in 1862 to allow
road widening. Queen
Street as a whole was only
named such in 1886 -
originally the name referred
to just one small section of
Crockerton (sometimes
'Crockherbtown'). In 1855
this short row inside the
town walls was described as
'merely a lane' containing
about 24 houses.

▶ **CARDIFF**
*Queen Street
1902* 48997

With a new
century and a
population
nearing 165,000
the town
increasingly gains
the trappings
of modernity.
The electric tram
is in its first year
of operation - a
generating station
on Newport Road
provides power.
A small group
gather beneath
the ornate canopy
of the Andrews
Hotel (right)
whilst of all the
signage apparent
in the street
'Morgan Painless
Dentistry' is
perhaps the most
dubious!

◀ **CARDIFF**
Queen Street 2004
C23733k

Years of wholesale
redevelopment have
rendered this view almost
unrecognisable as the
same street in 48997
(above). Our only clue is
the upper frontage of
Principles. The retention
of mature trees has
helped soften the vast
expanse of new paving
whilst the construction of
new retail premises
(right) underlines
Cardiff's status as one of
Britain's foremost
shopping destinations.

▲ **CARDIFF,** *The Hayes looking towards Working Street 1925* 77426

With its distinctive BO number plate we know that the car on the right was registered in Cardiff. But what of its driver? Perhaps he's going to enjoy an alcoholic beverage in the British Volunteer pub or take refreshment in David Morgan's lavish Japanese Tea Room. In the mid 1920s David Morgan proudly proclaimed that its ground floor windows (left) at 312ft were the 'longest continuous frontage' in the provinces.

◄**CARDIFF**
The Hayes looking towards Working Street 2004 C23721k

The upper façade of David Morgan appears unchanged but time is up for the Cardiff store. Once sold, the premises are tipped to house a supermarket and its grand upper floors will probably become residential space. The dated 1960s architecture of Oxford House opposite faces demolition - clearance of the Hayes/Bridge Street site is scheduled to make way for a vast new retail complex.

CARDIFF
St John's Church 1893
32682

The origin of St John's tower is not entirely clear. Following enlargement of the church (c1453-73) the construction of the distinctive 'West Country' type tower is believed to have been the gift of Lady Isabel, Duchess of Clarence. The work of possible architect John Hart on Bristol's St Stephen's Church is remarkably similar but stylistic details are also shared with the Jasper Tower of Llandaff Cathedral.

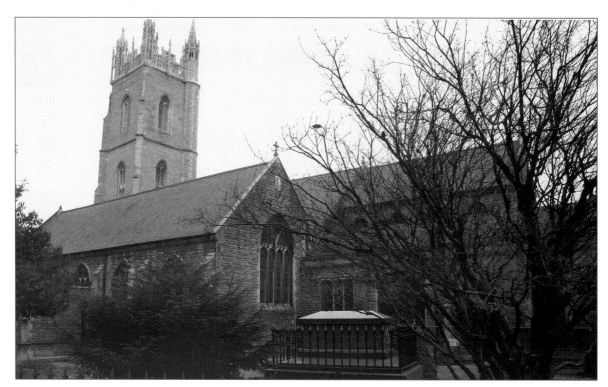

CARDIFF, *St John's Church 2004* C23724k

St John's stands virtually unchanged from 32682 (above). But for a small section of the castle, the church remains the only tangible link with the old town's medieval past. Golden masonry radiant in the sunshine and the cool green shade of the old cemetery make the area a city centre oasis. It now even boasts a café popular with both workers and tourists alike.

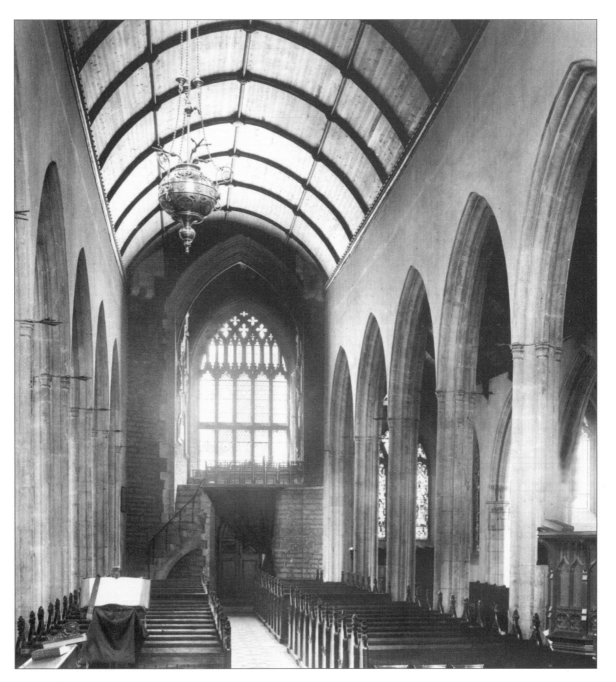

CARDIFF, *St Johns Church, the Interior 1893* 32684

The church interior is pictured here only four years after completion of extensive restoration work. Public subscription covered its £12,000 cost. Displaying characteristic taste and restraint John Prichard, the diocesan architect, left the medieval tower untouched but sympathetically added a vestry and extra aisles. Up to 1,500 worshippers could now sit bathed in the light from the beautiful stained glass windows.

CARDIFF, *Church Street 1925* 77429

This busy conduit linking St John's and High Street affords a perfect view of the tower. The old corner house (right) is occupied by Hope Brothers General Outfitters whilst opposite, as for many years, stands Oliver's Shoes. Welsh Sports Ltd began its long tenure in the street during this period. Those seeking other recreational pursuits could choose either the Old Dolphin or Old Arcade hostelries.

CARDIFF, *Church Street 2004* C23725k

The same church view as in 77429 but much else has changed. The old corner house boasts restored architectural features whilst the street's long-standing resident, the Old Arcade, has its frontage opened and modernised - the market entrance passage still intact. The thoroughfare now pedestrian, the laying of its Chinese granite cobbles marked the initiation of the city centre repaving programme.

CARDIFF
Kingsway c1960 C23144

This is the main automotive route north from the city centre yet pedestrians appear happy to saunter UP the road rather than across it! The sunken car park (left) and the railings (right) provide a visible clue to the course of the old canal tunnel. The imposing Prudential Building (right) had amongst its varied occupants manufacturers and fitters of artificial limbs - demand sadly increased by recent wars.

CARDIFF
Kingsway 2004
C23774k

A very familiar sight of buses, shelters and expectant passengers. The road layout remains but the old canal tunnel is now a useful pedestrian underpass. The building (right), vertically extended and modernised, is now the luxury Hilton Hotel. Beyond the hotel in the mid distance is an oddity - office space not yet fully let in the booming capital of the 21st century.

CARDIFF, *The Friary Ruins, Cathays Park c1955* C23077

Greyfriars House was built for William Herbert c1570 utilising the old Franciscan friary on the site as a quarry, the friary having been closed at the Dissolution. The mansion fell into ruin itself by the late 18th century. The endeavours of the third and fourth Marquesses saw the site excavated, footings laid out and eventually fenced in as a public space. Thus protected from the construction of Greyfriars Road Cardiffians believed that the site and its ruin were forever preserved.

CARDIFF, *Site of the Old Friary Ruins 2004* C23735k

The highly controversial sale of the site around 1960 resulted in the demolition of the ruins and the construction of the towering Pearl Assurance building in 1967. Now named the Capital Tower the passing years have diminished the shock of its size and scale with its dominance of the city skyline challenged by more recent building projects.

► **CARDIFF**
Cardiff Arms Park c1960
C23182

The Taff-side home of the famous 'Blue & Blacks'. The club forming in 1876, the ground took its name from the nearby Cardiff Arms Hotel demolished in 1878. Summer would find Glamorgan's cricketers running its well-manicured turf. Such was the fame of the club ground that to rugby fans the world over its name and that of the National Stadium were virtually synonymous.

◄**CARDIFF**
Millennium Stadium 2004 C23713k

The stadium, with its distinctive skyline masts, is perhaps the only modern construction in the city whose image can boast international recognition. This is due in part to its role as the current host of the FA Cup final - a match screened worldwide. Built for the 1999 Rugby World Cup it has a capacity almost 50% greater than the old National Stadium.

▲ **CARDIFF,** *The Park Hotel 1893* 32679

Opened in 1883 on the site of the old Crockherbtown Theatre, with money raised by a consortium headed by James Howell, the Park Hotel 'designed for high-class family business', was to epitomise the grandeur of Victorian travel and accommodation. Of its original shop units the prestigious corner site is here occupied by Penfold Brothers Bootmakers & Hatters.

◀**CARDIFF**
The Park Hotel 2004
C23732k

The hotel, acquired by the Thistle Group in 1996, has changed outwardly very little. Park Street taxi rank still operates but is no longer equine! The upper level façade is almost identical to that in 32679 (above) - a design strikingly similar to that of the Louvre gallery in Paris. Nowadays, the hotel faces a host of modern competitors in the city's luxury accommodation market.

► **CARDIFF**
The Library 1896
38710

A bust of Minerva sits proudly atop the grand Hayes façade of the library extension, probably pictured at the time of its opening in 1896. Interior space was at a premium - the premises included a museum and schools of both Art and Science. Established in 1882 in its first purpose-built home, the early adoption of the Free Library concept stood testament to Cardiff's municipal pride and foresight.

◄ **CARDIFF**
The Library 2004
C23722k

Since relinquishing its role as Central Library in 1988 the beautifully restored building, now dubbed the Old Library, has had a chequered history. Transformation into the Centre for the Visual Arts proved short-lived - its closing recriminations equal to that of its opening fanfare. Apart from an in-house pub, temporary exhibitions are its main occupants with the Cardiff Visitor Centre perhaps finding a fitting and permanent home.

▲ **CARDIFF,** *St David's Hall 2004* C23723k

Like much 1970s architecture, the building's façade has not aged particularly well. Its gauche exterior, however, belies the superb auditorium of this self-proclaimed 'National Concert Hall of Wales'. Rightly regarded as a first class venue it plays host to the whole spectrum of musical styles. The annual staging of the prestigious 'Cardiff Singer of the World' contest has bestowed an international profile.

◄**CARDIFF**
*International Arena
2004* C23719k

Opened by the Queen in 1993 the Cardiff International Arena is described by its owners as the 'complete venue'. Its facilities are certainly impressive. Many will be familiar with its role as a 5,500-seat concert venue but the vast events complex was also designed to house a wide selection of corporate and conference suites and the globally-linked Cardiff World Trade Centre.

CARDIFF CASTLE
AND SOPHIA GARDENS

CARDIFF, *The Castle, South Side 1893* 32670

The Animal Wall is seen here in its original location.
Among the first creatures delivered were the sealion,
lynx and monkeys. Also in situ by 1888 were the lions
bearing the Bute arms positioned on either side of the
main gate. Deemed unsatisfactory by the Marquess for
apparently looking 'too modest in demeanour' their
subsequent return for retouching did little to change
their docile appearance.

CARDIFF
The Castle, South Side
c1903 32670a

A charming illustration of the changing face of public transport in the city. At left, a modern wonder on route to St Mary Street - electric trams were introduced into service only a year earlier. At right, a group of fashionable ladies stroll towards a traditional horse bus. This mode of carriage provided transport from the Castle Gate to Llandaff as late as the First World War.

CARDIFF, *The Castle, South Side 2004* C23776k

Although the castle entrance is enlarged, the Animal Wall re-sited and the trailing vines long since removed, this remains a familiar scene. A busy thoroughfare still but horses and tramlines have long vanished. The motorbus was introduced into the city c1920 and a stationary open top example (left) awaits the next party of inquisitive tourists and sightseers.

41

CARDIFF, *The Castle Clock Tower c1960* C23147

The Clock Tower, constructed during the extensive restoration and alteration of the castle 1867-72, was a Burges-designed monument to the third Marquess and his extended family. Each side not only carries astronomical and astrological themed statues but also inset shields positioned immediately above the clock faces. The five on each side depict the familial arms of Herbert, Crichton, Stuart, Montague and Windsor.

CARDIFF
The Castle from Bute Park c1960
C23218

Although partially obscured by foliage this view admirably shows the historical reinvention of the Castle and, in particular, its western façade. The four towers we see here illustrate 400 years of change from the turreted Herbert Tower of the early 18th century (second from left) to the 'high Victorian dream' of Burges' late 19th century Clock Tower on the extreme right.

CARDIFF, *Sophia Gardens 1896* 38711

Sophia Gardens can be regarded as the city's first public park. In 1857, prompted by continental initiatives, the widow of the second Marquess resolved to set 'a noble example to other towns' and present the people with a pleasure ground of 'exquisite taste and design'. Although popular with the citizens, the Butes' motives and retention of ownership were initially met with scepticism and suspicion.

◄ **CARDIFF**
*Sophia Gardens
Pavilion c1960* C23171

Despite suffering a reputation for poor acoustics this much loved venue played host to many of the greatest names in popular music from the 1950s to the late 1970s. Built originally as part of Cardiff's contribution to the 1951 Festival of Britain, time was eventually to catch up with the pavilion. A heavy snowfall in January 1982 caused its roof to collapse leading to the eventual demolition of the building.

CARDIFF
Sophia Gardens
c1950 C23057

The park would not officially belong to the people until September 1947. The land, along with 150 acres of Bute Park, would generously supplement the fifth Marquess' 'gift' of Cardiff Castle to its citizens. A day of massive celebration, the like of which had not been seen in the city for many years, marked its acceptance into Cardiff Corporation ownership.

CARDIFF
Welsh Institute of
Sport 2004 C23763k

Following a two-year building programme, the £670,000 National Sports Centre opened in 1971 on a site near the Pavilion - the culmination of a ten-year effort to create a central home for Welsh sport's governing bodies. Now fully refurbished and renamed Welsh Institute of Sport, the Sophia Gardens-based complex provides first class indoor facilities for amateur and professional alike.

THE CIVIC
CENTRE

CARDIFF
City Hall and Law Courts 1906 54938

Admired by a lady sitting in the area later to be
occupied by the National Museum stands the City Hall,
a year after the bestowal of Cardiff's city status. The
move to locate the then Town Hall out of the 'old town'
was considered bold and proved contentious. Objectors
to the audacious scheme suggested alternative sites in
the Arms Park and Temperance Town.

CARDIFF
City Hall and Law Courts 2004 C23743k

A call to house the Welsh Assembly rejected, City Hall still 'belongs' to its citizens. Regarded as 'a fine building looking for use' its role as an administrative centre has greatly diminished since the formation of the new unitary authority. With County Hall having absorbed much of its function, it increasingly performs more of a ceremonial role in civic matters.

CARDIFF, *City Hall 1925* 77437

Today's motorists can but marvel at the wide expanse of road on offer here. The formal layout of roads around the Civic Centre was initiated in 1903 some five years after completion of the purchase of Bute's parkland. Original plans for one grand avenue leading from Queen Street to City Hall proved fruitless - a development partially hindered by the Bute retention of the adjacent Greyfriars site.

CARDIFF
The National Museum of Wales c1950 C23062

Brimming with civic pride and vastly superior finances the city pushed hard to house both the National Library and Museum. The former lost to Aberystwyth, the lure of a prime, freely available site helped to eclipse all rival museum bids. Thus won for the city, the construction of a National Museum of Wales was a prolonged affair - 15 years from foundation stone to official opening.

CARDIFF, *County Hall c1960* C23221

The opening in 1912 of the County Hall in Cathays Park provided a much-needed centrally contained administrative centre for Glamorgan. The classically proportioned building complete with Corinthian columns was executed in a neo-Grecian style. The statues flanking its main entrance steps portray mining and nautical navigation themes - both endeavours vital to the prosperity of the city and county.

CARDIFF
County Hall 2004
C23740k

The reorganisation of the old Glamorgan County eventually resulted in the building being used somewhat incongruously as the headquarters of Mid Glamorgan County Council - a cuckoo in the Cardiff civic nest. University College took over the premises in the late 1990s and it is now perhaps best known for housing the Glamorgan Record Office.

CARDIFF, *The University 1902* 49001a

The opening of the University College of South Wales and Monmouthshire in 1883 was considered momentous enough to merit a public holiday. Located on Newport Road's old Infirmary site its £50,000 set-up cost was partially met by the Marquess of Bute. The initial student intake numbered 151 - female students significantly gaining entrance from the outset.

◄**CARDIFF**
*University College
2004* C23742k

The College, masonry pristine, is still the visual identity of academia in the city. Having celebrated its centenary in 1993 the University of Wales is the oldest of its kind in Europe. With the proposed merger with the College of Medicine (itself established in 1893) the new so called 'super' University will boast in excess of 39,000 students.

◄CARDIFF
University College
1925 77442

The 'new' University College building which opened in October 1909 was the fruition of ten years' concerted fundraising aided by the Corporation's gift of five acres of building land. Its unusually elongated frontage, allegedly imposed by height restrictions, proved controversial. Not so its library - the Caroe-designed Turner-built amenity was described as 'a dream in architecture' during its opening proceedings.

▲ **CARDIFF,** *The War Memorial c1950* C23058

Even before the end of the First World War calls had been made to erect a monument to honour Wales' dead. After years of fundraising initiated by the 'Western Mail' newspaper a war memorial was finally constructed in Cathays Park's Queen Alexandra Gardens. The Memorial was officially dedicated by the Bishop of Wales on 12 June 1928.

◄CARDIFF
The War Memorial
2004 C23739k

Visually unaltered, the memorial is still the focus of remembrance in the city. The original Book Of Remembrance containing the names of 35,000 fallen is now overshadowed by the death tolls of conflicts unimaginable to those at its original presentation. The statues of the soldier, sailor and airman holding wreathes aloft bear silent witness to the city's and the nation's sacrifice.

INTO
THE SUBURBS

CARDIFF
St Mary's Church, the Interior 1899 43602

The new St Mary's on Bute Street opened in 1843 but was
completed the following year. Money raised by public
subscription barely covered the building cost of its two
towers. Not until the second Marquess was able to buy,
then sell, what remained of the original St Mary's Taff-
side site, would sufficient funds be made available to
finance this spiritual centre of his eponymous Butetown.

CARDIFF
*St Saviour's Church,
the Interior 1899* 43601

St Saviour's has remained a constant in the changing urban landscape of Splott's main commercial thoroughfare. Built to a design by G F Bradley it is reputedly closely based on a church in Tenby. With the foundation stone laid by Lord Tredegar, consecration took place just nine months later in October 1888. For years its candle-lit carol services have occupied a special place in the hearts of local schoolchildren.

CARDIFF, *The Infirmary 1893* 32681

Opened in 1883 the Edward Seward-designed South Wales and Monmouthshire Infirmary was built at a cost of £23,000. Replacing much smaller and increasingly inadequate local facilities dating back to the 1830s, the requisite funds came in from across the social spectrum. Wealthy individuals, Cardiff Corporation, miners' subscriptions and even the church collection plate all contributed to its upkeep.

▶ **CARDIFF**
Newport Road
2004 C23707k

The main route into
the city from the east
is a fine illustration of
the refurbishment
and diversification of
redundant 1960s
office space. Beyond
St James' Church and
the scaffolded former
GPO building stands
the most indicative.
The city has gained
another luxury hotel,
the Macdonald
Holland, housed in
the shell of what was
originally the Julian
Hodge building.

◀ **CARDIFF**
Llanrumney Hall,
Llanrumney Estate
c1960 C23188

In its time Llanrumney
Hall (right) has been the
property of both the
Morgans of Tredegar and
the Williams family of
Roath Court. In 1952 the
house and grounds were
bought by the City
Council. Ownership of
the house itself was a
bonus as acquisition of
its large estate was the
primary motivation. The
vast parkland was to
provide much-needed
house building space.

▲ **CARDIFF,** *Llanrumney Estate c1960* C23187

The possibility of re-housing in the green open spaces of the Llanrumney estates was an extremely attractive proposition for families more used to the cramped inner city. The post war building programme had originally been facilitated by the Cardiff Extension Act of 1937 allowing the city to expand eastwards pushing Glamorgan's boundary past the River Rumney and into areas hitherto part of Monmouthshire.

◄**CARDIFF**
Llanrumney Estate
2004 C23702k

With the development of St Mellons, Trowbridge and most recently Pontprennau, Cardiff and Newport move geographically closer. Llanrumney has long ceased to be the city's eastern outer edge. Its newness diminished, the estate has matured, retaining much of its greenery and open aspect. It remains a popular residential suburb.

► **CARDIFF**
*Maindy Stadium
c1960* C23164

By the early 1960s memories of Maindy Stadium's relatively inauspicious opening in 1951 and, in particular, its poor running track surface were all but banished. Large crowds now flocked to the venue, their appetite for quality athletics meets whetted by the success of the city's hosting of the Empire Games in 1958 and the subsequent establishment of the Welsh Sports Council in 1959.

◄ **CARDIFF**
Fidlas Road c1965
C23240

Then, as now, Rhydypennau crossroads was a thriving commercial intersection at which three north eastern suburbs meet - Llanishen to our right, Cyncoed to our left and Heath straight ahead through the railway arches. Just out of picture at right is the tiny kiosk renowned locally for its Sunday opening - a rarity at this time and a perfect place for ice cream on route to Roath Park.

▲ **CARDIFF,** *St David's Hospital 2004* C23709k

Originally constructed in the 1830s Cardiff Union Workhouse was the first significant public building of the Canton/Riverside area. Becoming St David's Hospital in 1923 it served for many years as the prime source of healthcare for West Cardiff's inner suburbs. Closure led to neglect and partial destruction by fire. Its restored façade now fronts a small new medical facility and residential development.

◀ **CARDIFF**
Victoria Park c1965
C23210

Created by the acquisition of land once part of Ely Common, Victoria Park was opened on the occasion of the monarch's Diamond Jubilee in 1897. It became the perfect western counterpart to Roath Park in the east that had opened almost exactly three years earlier. Long associated with the exploits of Billy the Seal the park even housed its own small zoo until 1941.

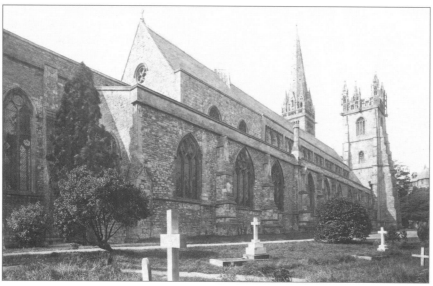

◀ **LLANDAFF**
The Cathedral from the North-East 1893
32700

After a prolonged period of restoration Llandaff Cathedral was reopened during Easter 1857. Unlike in previous eras, the architects overseeing the mid 19th-century work were determined to respect the medieval origins of the building. The vagaries of hundreds of years of changing architectural fashion had left the cathedral with a myriad of conflicting structural and decorative alterations.

◄ **CARDIFF**
*Victoria Park
2004* C23764k

1997 saw the park mark its centenary in style with celebrations that recalled its Victorian origins. A replica of the bandstand - absent since the 1950s - was unveiled and Billy the Seal was immortalised in sculpture. With a massive replanting programme set to recreate its original horticultural splendour, last year's Green Flag award for excellence came as little surprise.

◄ **LLANDAFF**
*The Cathedral from the
North-East 2004*
C23744k

Despite 80 years of Anglican disestablishment the cathedral remains a religious focal point for Cardiffians. The devastating bombing raid of 1941 necessitated a new time of reconstruction guided to completion by George Pace in 1964. The modernist spirit of the work is here apparent in the addition of the Welch Regiment Memorial Chapel's stylishly curved façade delicately faced with river pebbles (right).

LLANDAFF, *The Cathedral, the West Front c1874* 7038

The main burden of contemporary criticism lay with the Cathedral's West Front. Whereas Prichard's work on the 15th century Jasper Tower was very much in tune with the prevailing conservative medieval taste his South Tower (c1867), with open parapet and tall octagonal spire, was regarded as a radical innovation lending the façade an unusually asymmetric look.

LLANDAFF
The Cathedral Nave, looking East 1893 32703

By 1861, reconstruction work virtually complete, Prichard and partners had overseen the fourth rebuilding of the cathedral. A new Clerestory was added, ruined arcades renewed and an open timbered roof constructed over the Nave (pictured here). Prichard's work proved controversial amongst his peers. Leading 'medievalist' architects and devotees, including William Burges, were unimpressed and quick to voice their misgivings in print.

LLANDAFF, *The Cathedral Nave, Looking East 2004* C23777k

The ceiling now flat and simplistically-timbered, the interior is now dominated by Epstein's 'Majestas'. The magnificent aluminium figure is mounted on a bold concrete arch with the cylindrical organ case, itself adorned with large Pre-Raphaelite figures. These once stood in the niches of the choir stalls and, unlike much contemporary interior decoration, survived the landmine dropped near the South Wall.

ROATH PARK

CARDIFF, *Roath Park 1896* 38713

A view evoking the sheer scale of the 130-acre park. The size of the project would make the development extremely expensive and provoked much contemporary criticism. Grand schemes were to be tempered by financial reality. The 'Wild Garden' northern section of the park was planned to house a second lake - lack of funds put paid to this and the area remained as found.

CARDIFF
Roath Park 1896
38714

The marvellously rustic bridge over the Brook in the Pleasure Gardens. The 11-acre site south of the main park was laid out so that 'old folk and children' may enjoy the 'odours' and 'admire in quietness' the beauty of the flowers. A guide to the park (c1905) claimed that water voles and trout were present along this stretch.

CARDIFF, *Roath Park 1931* C23053

Often referred to by locals as the 'Flower Gardens' here is the same scene some 35 years after that shown in 38714 (above) and a new concrete bridge is in place. In the distance the encroaching modern era is further evident by the tennis courts and bowling green - both installed around the time of the First World War.

CARDIFF
Roath Park Lake 1896
38715

Ignoring the small building (left) and the iron railings this could almost be a rural scene. Pictured here only two years after opening, the lake, created from a 'malarial bog' by damming the Nant Fawr Brook, proved extremely problematic. Excavation work was further hindered by floods arising from hillside springs on land east of the park.

65

CARDIFF
Roath Park 2004
C23759k

Today, rowing boats are not permitted near any of the lake's 'bird islands'. Along with the lake embankment the islands were constructed from excavated soil. It's interesting to note that the southern end of the lake, pictured here, is approximately 14ft deep whereas the northern part around the islands is extremely shallow - a mere 2ft deep in places.

CARDIFF, *Roath Park Lake 1902* 49000x

Note the symmetry of this early residential development on Lake Road East with its grand row of houses book-ended by conical towers. Balconies afford superb views across the lake for some of Cardiff's wealthiest inhabitants. On our left, in the distance, open land has yet to be developed into suburban Cyncoed. The right of picture shows Cefn Coed Road under construction.

▲ CARDIFF
Roath Park Lake 1902
49001

It's quite possible that the attendant pictured here is the much-loved 'Sammy the Boatman'. Described as 'the friend of the children of Cardiff' in his touching 'Western Mail' obituary, the Norwegian-born Mr Stephenson superintended bathing for 31 years. He died in 1933 aged 79. It was said that the sound of his whistle would cause birds to flock to eat out of his hand.

◀ *detail from* 49001

CARDIFF
Roath Park Lake 1925
77445

With smartly-dressed attendants very much in evidence we may be viewing an early morning scene as the boats are lined up and ready but there are few paying customers. The huts to the left of the picture already look slightly past their best. Note the open vista through the trees at the top left of photograph - the park not yet fully encircled by housing.

CARDIFF
Roath Park Lake
2004 C23756k

Pride of place is now the award-winning structure built to provide shelter for the boats and an excellent platform from which to view the lake. Our gentleman attendants in photograph 77445 (page 68-69) would no doubt be in approval of the traditional rowing boats in use but one can only guess their reaction if confronted by the 'Duck Paddlers' in the enclosed children's area!

CARDIFF, *Roath Park Lake 1925* 77444

The rowing boat in front of the lighthouse seems almost as fully laden as the motor launch 'Britannia' in the foreground! Since the park's inception the provision of pleasure boats has proved a major attraction. The Parks Committee initially made 50 vessels available - ten different contractors supplying five boats each. This move coincided with the appointment of the first five park keepers.

CARDIFF, *Roath Park 1931* C23056

The bathing stage at the lake's eastern edge reminds us of how popular swimming once was. Up to 35,000 bathers per season made use of the supervised facility. The lake played host to the 'Taff Swim' from 1931 - the river itself was considered too polluted. Sadly, swimming in the lake was prohibited in 1962. Years of silting and pollution had taken its toll.

CARDIFF
Roath Park 2004
C23761k

In recent years the poor visual appearance of the lake became somewhat a 'cause celebre'. Extensive improvement work has rectified this. Silt has been removed from around the islands and most of the waterweed cleared from its surface - its unsightliness belying its role as a rich source of food for fish and fowl. Both populations (especially the swans) are thriving.

CARDIFF, *The Promenade, Roath Park 1955* C23099

Prior to the advent of mass car ownership cycling to the park was an even more popular option than today. With so many bicycles present this busy scene is more reminiscent of Oxford or Cambridge. Indentification of one's own on retrieval must have proved challenging! Note how neglected the Scott Memorial appears, its faded grey colour unfamiliar to us today.

CARDIFF, *The Promenade, Roath Park 2004* C23758k

The 'bicycle corner' has now given way to the extended terrace of the Terra Nova Café. This refreshment area overlooks the landing stage for the lake's 12-berth motor launch 'Roath's Pride'. After its recent £4,000 overhaul the lighthouse looks immaculate. Amongst the work undertaken was the renovation of the weather-damaged clock face and full restoration of its internal mechanism.

THE DOCKS AND CARDIFF BAY

CARDIFF, *The Docks 1893* 32697

It is virtually impossible to overstate the role of the docks in the prosperity of the city. The entrance of the 'Lady Charlotte' steamer into Bute West Dock (Cardiff's first enclosed system) in 1839 heralded a staggering new era of trade. Capacity increased by completion of Bute East in 1859. Roath Dock officially opened in 1887, with the Queen Alexandra Dock the last to be opened in 1907.

CARDIFF
*Great Western Offices
1925* 77413

The rich terracotta brick
Pier Head building (right)
was constructed in 1886 as
offices for the Bute Dock
Company. Some claim that
the grandeur of its design
vershadowed that of the
Coal Exchange prompting
the latter's overhaul and
refurbishment in 1911. In
1922 it was taken over by
the Great Western Railway
whose acquisition of every
South Wales port instantly
made them the world's
largest dock owner.

◀ **CARDIFF**
Bute Docks 1925 77423

A paddle steamer momentarily obscures Penarth Head on route to Cardiff where it will join the massed ranks of vessels from all around the world. It is perhaps difficult today to appreciate the port's international standing at this time. Just prior to the First World War nearly 50 nations had consular representatives based in the area - sometimes a single person acting on behalf of two small neighbouring countries.

◀ **CARDIFF**
Pier Head 2004
C23714k

A perfect juxtaposition of old and new. The beautifully-restored Pier Head building is flanked by Roald Dahl's Plass (Oval Basin) and the stylish leisure and retail facilities of Mermaid Quay - all products of periods of economic boom. At right, the awesome Millennium Centre nears completion. This is the modern landmark building the Bay sorely needs after the Opera House fiasco.

◀ **CARDIFF**
Bute Docks, now the Marina 2004 c23717k

Today the city's international reputation is based on its leisure and tourist facilities. The former tidal basin is now a fresh water lake. A waterbus (centre) enables exploration of its eight-mile waterfront. The St David's Hotel & Spa (second from right) was completed along with the barrage in 1999. With its distinctively futuristic roof structure it is Cardiff's first purpose built five star hotel.

► **CARDIFF**
The Docks c1955
C23102

Visiting international vessels not withstanding, the docks were slipping into an inexorable decline during an otherwise glorious time for the city with capital status officially recognised. 1956 would herald the end of Cardiff as a fishing port and, even more devastatingly, its last coal shipment would leave just eight years later.

◄ CARDIFF
Bute Docks 1925 77418

Since the halcyon days of 1913 the docks' export tonnage was in steady decline, recovering briefly during the fuel demand of the First World War.1925 was to prove a fateful year for the port. Churchill's decision to return Britain to the Gold Standard of 1914 instantly made Welsh coal much more expensive than that of its competitors - effectively pricing it out of the market.

◄**CARDIFF**
County Hall 2004
C23779k

To demonstrate its belief
in the viability of a
redeveloped waterfront
the County Council
relocated its headquarters
in 1988. Thus the £28
million 'Giant Pagoda'
became the first
significant building of the
new Cardiff Bay.
To improve access an
adjacent peripheral
distributor road was
constructed - the dual
carriageway vital for rapid
transport from inner city
to southern edge.

◀ **CARDIFF**
The Docks c1960 C23156

A new decade would usher in an era of rapid decline. Both Bute East and West docks neared closure. West finally succumbed in 1964 with East surviving a further six years. The famous Butetown community was ripped apart by a programme of demolition and re-housing. We now know that the area was not dead but merely dormant.

◀**CARDIFF**
National Assembly 2004
C23711k

Crickhowell House originally opened in 1993 and has, since 1999, played temporary host to the National Assembly whilst the greatly delayed new debating chamber is constructed. The use of Crickhowell House itself has proved controversial, with Rhodri Morgan once calling into question its construction standards and the financial expediency of its occupation.

CARDIFF
The Bay Barrage 2004
C23769k

With the destruction of important wildlife habitats by flooding, the completion of the barrage proved the most controversial aspect of the bay development. Environmental concerns aside the costly futuristic structure is stunning. The construction impounds the rivers Taff and Ely but three navigation locks allow through traffic - the largest able to manage 12 yachts at a time.

CARDIFF
The Marina Entrance 2004 C23768k

It is entirely appropriate that the Marina is depicted in the last photograph in our selection. As early as 1977 the then South Glamorgan County Council realised that a priority for Cardiff was the 'industrial expansion, redevelopment and reclamation of the waterfront strip'. The formation of the Cardiff Bay Development Corporation in 1987 led to the transformation of the neglected area that accounted for nearly ten percent of the city. Now a major tourist attraction the waterfront is home to numerous popular bars, restaurants and cafes. The development of residential areas continues apace but even their staunchest supporters agree that they have yet to gel as communities. With the breathtaking changes to the city over the past 20 years it will perhaps take another 20 before we can accurately assess the re-birth of Europe's self-proclaimed 'youngest capital. Watch this space!

INDEX

NAMES OF SUBSCRIBERS

The following people have kindly supported this book by subscribing to copies before publication.

E C Agar, Cardiff

Mrs Sylvia Airey

Mr M A & Mrs B E Andrews, Cardiff

The Bailey Family: UK, NZ & USA

Mark Robert Bell

Ann Blake, Cardiff

Francine Bousfield

Colin Brinkworth

Kay & Dave Bullen, Cardiff

Shomola Burrell

Mr & Mrs F Calford & Family, Cardiff

Sue Chadwick, Rhiwbina

Tony & Lynda Chappell, Cardiff

The Chivell Family

Harry O M Coleman, Cardiff

To my Mum, Mrs Sandra Coles x

Mr A P & Mrs B Cronin, Cardiff

William Cross

Loretta Davies

Sandra Davies, 'Happy Birthday', love Mark

Mr & Mrs H N Davies, Cardiff

Capt & Mrs J Downard, formerly of Cardiff

Lance Edwards, Aberdare to Cardiff

Maurice Elliott

Mavis Ruth Elliott

Mr A & Mrs S Fowler, Cardiff

The Gibbs Family, Cardiff

Mr & Mrs R Gibbs, Cardiff

Mr M J Harris, Cardiff

J D Hegarty, Cardiff

The Heslop Family

Mr A Higginson, Birchgrove, Cardiff

Elaine Hill, Cardiff

In memory of Thomas Hoare, Portsmouth

Philip J Hughes, Cardiff

The Humphries Family

Mrs G Ireland and Catherine & Nicola

To Jean & Bernard from the staff 2004

The Jenkins Family, Cardiff

To John Jenkins, Taffs Well for Christmas

Mr Glyn Jones

Brian, Bridget & Hannah Joyce, Cardiff

In memory of E Karagianis, Cardiff

Very Special Grandparents - Mr & Mrs Kukla

Mr M E Ling & Mrs W Ling, Cardiff

Christopher K McIlquham, Cardiff 2004

Margaret & Family, Nantgarw, Cardiff

To Jean Morgan, love from the family xx

Jack Oliver Nicholas - A Fabulous Son

Nick

Glyn Nicoll

In memory of R D Nurton, Cardiff

Mr Graham Parker

Kenneth Parsons, Cardiff

Andrew Pearce

Michael Pearce

Stephen Pearce

Mark, Claire & Harrison Phillips, Cardiff

Mr R J & Mrs J L Phillips, Cardiff

Mr A C Porter & Mrs E A Porter, Cardiff

The Porter Family, Cardiff

Keith & Mollie Powell, Lisvane, Cardiff

Joan & Viv Purchase and Family

Daniel Rees and Family

Nathan & Matthew Roberts, Cardiff

Mr G G & Mrs P F Robinson

For Roger at Christmas 2004, from Mum

Dennis A Rose, Heath, Cardiff

C H & J I Rose, Whitchurch, Cardiff

In memory of D Ruperti, Cardiff

The Stone Family of Cardiff

Mr Stephen James Tatnell, Cardiff

Mr J A Thomas, Cardiff

Kenneth Thomas

Mr Mark Thomas

Mr & Mrs A Wade, Roath, Cardiff

Brian Wade, Cardiff

Helen Williams, Cardiff

Miss O V Williams, Rhiwbina

In memory of G Thomson Williams, Canton

Roy & Molly Willis and Family, Cardiff

Dennis P Willmott, Cardiff

In memory of Gordon Yates - A Super Dad, NY

R K Young, A C Young

FRITH PRODUCTS & SERVICES

Francis Frith would doubtless be pleased to know that the pioneering publishing venture he started in 1860 still continues today. Over a hundred and forty years later, The Francis Frith Collection continues in the same innovative tradition and is now one of the foremost publishers of vintage photographs in the world. Some of the current activities include:

Interior Decoration

Today Frith's photographs can be seen framed and as giant wall murals in thousands of pubs, restaurants, hotels, banks, retail stores and other public buildings throughout the country. In every case they enhance the unique local atmosphere of the places they depict and provide reminders of gentler days in an increasingly busy and frenetic world.

Product Promotions

Frith products are used by many major companies to promote the sales of their own products or to reinforce their own history and heritage. Frith promotions have been used by Hovis bread, Courage beers, Scots Porage Oats, Colman's mustard, Cadbury's foods, Mellow Birds coffee, Dunhill pipe tobacco, Guinness, and Bulmer's Cider.

Genealogy and Family History

As the interest in family history and roots grows world-wide, more and more people are turning to Frith's photographs of Great Britain for images of the towns, villages and streets where their ancestors lived; and, of course, photographs of the churches and chapels where their ancestors were christened, married and buried are an essential part of every genealogy tree and family album.

Frith Products

All Frith photographs are available Framed or just as Mounted Prints and Posters (size 23 x 16 inches). These may be ordered from the address below. From time to time other products - Address Books, Calendars, Table Mats, etc - are available.

The Internet

Already fifty thousand Frith photographs can be viewed and purchased on the internet through the Frith websites and a myriad of partner sites.

For more detailed information on Frith companies and products, look at these sites:

www.francisfrith.co.uk
www.francisfrith.com
(for North American visitors)

See the complete list of Frith Books at:

www.francisfrith.co.uk

This web site is regularly updated with the latest list of publications from the Frith Book Company. If you wish to buy books relating to another part of the country that your local bookshop does not stock, you may purchase on-line.

For further information, trade, or author enquiries please contact us at the address below:
The Francis Frith Collection, Frith's Barn, Teffont, Salisbury, Wiltshire, England SP3 5QP.
Tel: +44 (0)1722 716 376 Fax: +44 (0)1722 716 881   Email: sales@francisfrith.co.uk

See Frith books on the internet at www.francisfrith.co.uk

FREE PRINT OF YOUR CHOICE

Mounted Print
Overall size 14 x 11 inches (355 x 280mm)

Choose any Frith photograph in this book.
Simply complete the Voucher opposite and
return it with your remittance for £2.25 (to cover
postage and handling) and we will print the
photograph of your choice in SEPIA (size 11 x 8
inches) and supply it in a cream mount with a
burgundy rule line (overall size 14 x 11 inches).
**Please note: photographs with a reference
number starting with a "Z" are not Frith
photographs and cannot be supplied under
this offer.**
Offer valid for delivery to one UK address only.

PLUS: **Order additional Mounted Prints
at HALF PRICE - £7.49 each** (normally £14.99)
If you would like to order more Frith prints from
this book, possibly as gifts for friends and family,
you can buy them at half price (with no
additional postage and handling costs).

PLUS: **Have your Mounted Prints framed**
For an extra £14.95 per print you can have your
mounted print(s) framed in an elegant polished
wood and gilt moulding, overall size 16 x
13 inches (no additional postage and handling
required).

IMPORTANT!

These special prices are only available if you use
this form to order . You must use the ORIGINAL
VOUCHER on this page (no copies permitted). We
can only despatch to one UK address. This offer
cannot be combined with any other offer.

Send completed Voucher form to:
**The Francis Frith Collection, Frith's Barn,
Teffont, Salisbury, Wiltshire SP3 5QP**

CHOOSE A PHOTOGRAPH FROM THIS BOOK

Voucher for **FREE** and Reduced Price Frith Prints

*Please do not photocopy this voucher. Only the original is valid,
so please fill it in, cut it out and return it to us with your order.*

Picture ref no	Page no	Qty	Mounted @ £7.49	Framed + £14.95	Total Cost £
		1	Free of charge*	£	£
			£7.49	£	£
			£7.49	£	£
			£7.49	£	£
			£7.49	£	£
			£7.49	£	£

*Please allow 28 days
for delivery.
Offer available to one
UK address only*

* Post & handling	£2.25
Total Order Cost	£

Title of this book . . . .

I enclose a cheque/postal order for £ . . . .
made payable to 'The Francis Frith Collection'

OR please debit my Mastercard / Visa / Maestro / Amex
card, details below

Card Number

Issue No (Maestro only)   Valid from (Maestro)

Expires   Signature

Name Mr/Mrs/Ms . . . .
Address . . . .
. . . .
. . . .
. . . . Postcode . . . .
Daytime Tel No . . . .
Email . . . .

Valid to 31/12/07

Would you like to find out more about Francis Frith?

We have recently recruited some entertaining speakers who are happy to visit local groups, clubs and societies to give an illustrated talk documenting Frith's travels and photographs. If you are a member of such a group and are interested in hosting a presentation, we would love to hear from you.

Our speakers bring with them a small selection of our local town and county books, together with sample prints. They are happy to take orders. A small proportion of the order value is donated to the group who have hosted the presentation. The talks are therefore an excellent way of fundraising for small groups and societies.

Can you help us with information about any of the Frith photographs in this book?

We are gradually compiling an historical record for each of the photographs in the Frith archive. It is always fascinating to find out the names of the people shown in the pictures, as well as insights into the shops, buildings and other features depicted.

If you recognize anyone in the photographs in this book, or if you have information not already included in the author's caption, do let us know. We would love to hear from you, and will try to publish it in future books or articles.

Our production team

Frith books are produced by a small dedicated team at offices in the converted Grade II listed 18th-century barn at Teffont near Salisbury, illustrated above. Most have worked with the Frith Collection for many years. All have in common one quality: they have a passion for the Frith Collection. The team is constantly expanding, but currently includes:

Paul Baron, Phillip Brennan, Jason Buck, John Buck, Ruth Butler, Heather Crisp, David Davies, Louis du Mont, Isobel Hall, Gareth Harris, Lucy Hart, Julian Hight, Peter Horne, James Kinnear, Karen Kinnear, Tina Leary, Stuart Login, David Marsh, Lesley-Ann Millard, Sue Molloy, Glenda Morgan, Wayne Morgan, Sarah Roberts, Kate Rotondetto, Dean Scource, Eliza Sackett, Terence Sackett, Sandra Sampson, Adrian Sanders, Sandra Sanger, Jan Scrivens, Julia Skinner, David Smith, Miles Smith, Lewis Taylor, Shelley Tolcher, Lorraine Tuck, Amanita Wainwright and Ricky Williams.